W9-BDB-462

Basic Vocabulary™

Home

Al Bullock
Barbara Cleghorn
Margery Fraser
Paul Frewen
Pat Mills
Audrey Soutar

Skill Areas:	Vocabulary
Ages:	5 thru 11
Grades:	K thru 5

LinguiSystems

LinguiSystems, Inc.
3100 4th Avenue
East Moline, IL 61244-9700
1-800 PRO IDEA
1-800-776-4332

FAX: 1-800-577-4555
E-mail: service@linguisystems.com
Web: www.linguisystems.com
TDD: 1-800-933-8331
        (for those with hearing
         impairments)

Printed in the U.S.A.

ISBN 0-7606-0484-3

About the Authors

Front row: Paul Frewen, Barbara Cleghorn, Pat Mills
Back row: Margery Fraser, Al Bullock, Audrey Soutar

At the time of the writing of the *Basic Vocabulary* series, the authors were a group of six classroom teachers at inner-city schools in Ottawa, Ontario. Their teaching experiences range from kindergarten to eighth grade in a wide variety of schools and classroom situations. They have been involved in delivering regular graded programs to classes with extremely high percentages of English as a Second Language students. It is in this area that the authors are particularly qualified to assist other classroom teachers who require support for students at the beginning and middle levels of language acquisition.

Illustrations by Ken Prestley - Blue Sky Communications
Page Layout by Silver Oaks Communications
Cover Design by Lisa Parker

Table of Contents

Introduction

Basic Vocabulary – Home has been developed by classroom teachers for classroom teachers. It is intended to help students develop sight word vocabulary as they work independently or as part of a group. It can be used by students for vocabulary development, as well as for English as a Second Language instruction.

This book concentrates on one theme – Home. The vocabulary within the book progresses from simple to difficult, and words introduced in one unit might appear in later units to build your students' understanding of those words. Level 1 is for students ages 5 – 8. Level 2 is for students ages 8 – 11. Level 2 is divided into two parts. Part 1 is a review of the vocabulary introduced in Level 1. Part 2 introduces your students to new vocabulary related to the theme.

This practical, ready-to-use series requires little preparation and can be used alongside other programs. *Basic Vocabulary – Home* allows you to:

- provide your students with an immediately useful, sight-based vocabulary with a thematic approach

- provide a modified program to meet students' individual needs

- build language acquisition with individuals, small groups, and entire classrooms

The variety of activities and approaches used to address an array of learning styles and the simple directions allow you to send activity sheets home to involve parents. Students use writing, cutting and gluing, and visual recall to build their vocabulary. Also, each set of directions is written to the students so they can follow along as you read. Specific types of activities include:

Pictures in Context – Each unit begins by introducing the vocabulary in the context of a picture scene.

Words in Isolation – Students identify, match, read, write, and spell the sight vocabulary.

Sentence Completion – Students use their newly acquired vocabulary within correct syntax.

Following Directions – Students demonstrate comprehension skills by following directions.

The Extension Activities provide additional worksheets related to the theme. The Vocabulary Picture Cards can be copied or mounted onto heavier paper, cut apart, and colored by your students and used as flash cards. They can also be used to play Concentration or Lotto. You might also enlarge the individual pictures and have students place the cards on the actual items in your classroom (e.g., place the *desk* card on a desk).

The key to *Basic Vocabulary – Home* is its comprehensive, repetitive approach to new language acquisition and its flexibility to meet your needs. You choose which activities to use with your students and in what order they are to be completed. However you choose to use the materials in this book, though, we hope that you and your students work together to build better language and basic vocabulary skills.

Al, Barbara, Margery, Paul, Pat, and Audrey

Vocabulary List

Time/Calendar

afternoon	Hickory, Dickory, Dock	months	o'clock	time
clock	hour	morning	seconds	watch
day	midnight	night	special days	week
days of the week	minute	noon	spring	winter
fall	month	numbers	summer	year

In the Kitchen

cupboard	microwave
dishwasher	refrigerator
drawer	sink
kitchen	stove

In the Living Room

armchair	lamp
CD player	living room
couch	television
curtains	VCR
DVD player	

At the Table

bowl	mug
fork	napkin
glass	plate
knife	spoon

In the Bathroom

bathroom	toilet
bathtub	toothbrush
shower	towel
soap	washcloth

In the Bedroom

alarm clock	closet
bed	dresser
bedroom	mirror
blanket	pillow

Other Words Used

a	far	I	orange	see
an	from	in	out	the
are	gray	is	pink	this
black	green	near	purple	white
blue	have	of	red	yellow
brown	here			

Cut out these pages for the front and back covers of your calendar book.

Months of the Year

January	Jan.
February	Feb.
March	Mar.
April	Apr.
May	May
June	June
July	July
August	Aug.
September	Sept.
October	Oct.
November	Nov.
December	Dec.

Days of the Week

Sunday	Sun.
Monday	Mon.
Tuesday	Tues.
Wednesday	Wed.
Thursday	Thurs.
Friday	Fri.
Saturday	Sat.

Time/Calendar 1, cont.

Name _____

Make 12 copies of this calendar for your calendar book. Fill in the months and add numbers (dates). Also put any special days and holidays in the correct places.

_____

Sunday	Monday	Tuesday	Wednesday	Thursday	Friday	Saturday

Cut out the numbers at the bottom of the page and glue them in the correct places on the clock.

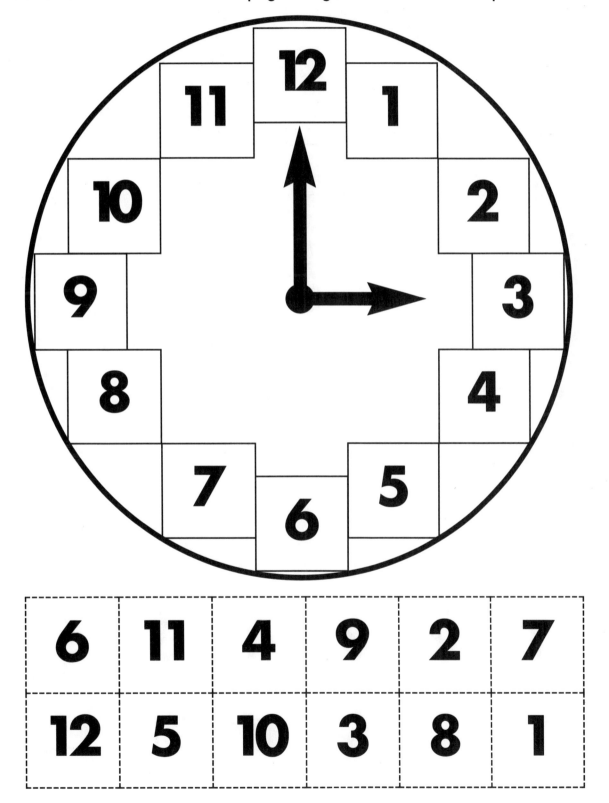

Name _____

Cut out the numbers at the bottom of the page and glue them in the correct places on the clock.

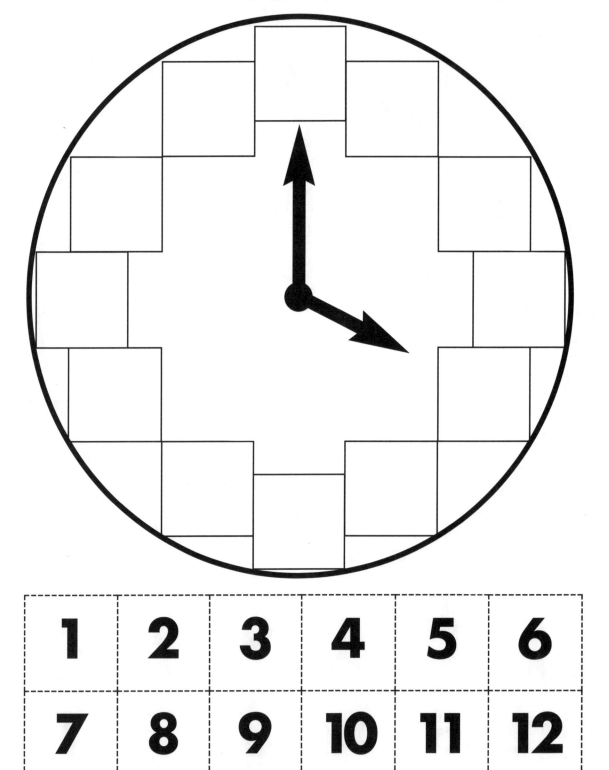

1	2	3	4	5	6
7	8	9	10	11	12

Complete each sentence.

Hickory, Dickory, Dock
Hickory, dickory, dock.
The mouse ran up the clock.
The clock struck one,
The mouse ran down.
Hickory, dickory, dock.

Hickory, Dickory, Dock

Hickory, dickory, _____,

The _____ ran up the _____.

The clock struck _____,

The mouse ran _____.

Hickory, _____, _____.

Time/Calendar 4

Print the number that tells what time it is. An example is done for you.

_4_ o'clock

___ o'clock

___ o'clock

___ o'clock

___ o'clock

___ o'clock

___ o'clock

___ o'clock

___ o'clock

___ o'clock

Time/Calendar 5

Print the number that tells what time it is. An example is done for you.

_2_ : 30

____ : 30

____ : 30

____ : 30

____ : 30

____ : 30

____ : 30

Time/Calendar 6

Draw hands on each clock to show what time it is.

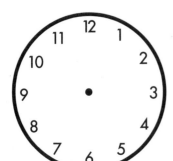

<u>2 o'clock</u>

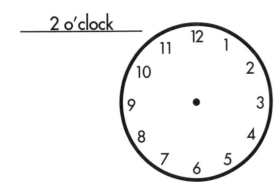

<u>6 o'clock</u>

<u>7:30</u>

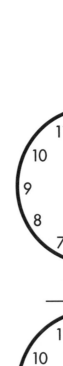

<u>1:30</u>

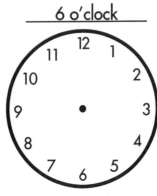

<u>11 o'clock</u>

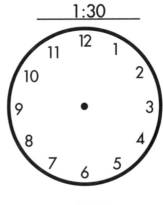

<u>12:30</u>

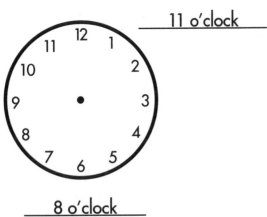

<u>8 o'clock</u>

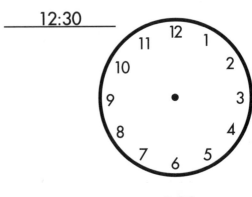

<u>9:30</u>

Draw a line to match each time with the correct clock.

6:00

10:00

3:00

12:30

10:30

7:30

2:30

8:30

4:30

Time/Calendar 8

Name _____

Draw hands on each clock to show the time.

| 9:00 |  | 9:30 | |

| 6:00 | | 7:30 | |

| 11:00 | | 11:30 | |

| 1:00 | | 1:30 | |

| 7:00 | | 3:30 | |

Time/Calendar 9

Circle what time you think it is in each picture.

12 o'clock
7 o'clock

8 o'clock
10 o'clock

10 o'clock
7 o'clock

3 o'clock
6 o'clock

10 o'clock
12 o'clock

9 o'clock
2 o'clock

Name _____

Print the number of days in each month. Then, print the month.

January	July
February	August
March	September
April	October
May	November
June	December

18

Print each month's abbreviation

January _____ ············· _____	July _____ ············· _____
February _____ ············· _____	August _____ ············· _____
March _____ ············· _____	September _____ ············· _____
April _____ ············· _____	October _____ ············· _____
May _____ ············· _____	November _____ ············· _____
June _____ ············· _____	December _____ ············· _____

Print the name of each day. Then, cut out each abbreviation and glue it by the correct day.

Wed.	Sat.	Thurs.	Tues.	Fri.	Sun.	Mon.

Sunday _____ ☐

Monday _____ ☐

Tuesday _____ ☐

Wednesday _____ ☐

Thursday _____ ☐

Friday _____ ☐

Saturday _____ ☐

Time/Calendar 13

Cut out the names of the days. Glue them in the correct order. Then, print the name of the day.

☐	_____
☐	_____
☐	_____
☐	_____
☐	_____
☐	_____
☐	_____

| Wednesday | Friday | Monday | Thursday | Saturday | Sunday | Tuesday |

Cut out each picture and glue it above the season it matches.

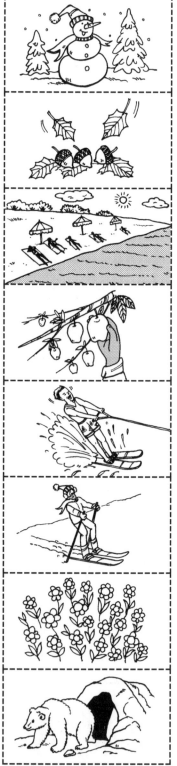

Summer

Fall

Winter

Spring

Name _____

Print each word.

morning

noon

afternoon

night

Time/Calendar 16

Print the days of the week in the boxes.

S				

M				

T					

W						

T						

F				

S						

Sunday

Monday   Thursday

Tuesday   Friday

Wednesday   Saturday

Name _____

Read the word for each object pictured.

kitchen

cupboard

microwave

stove

dishwasher

sink

refrigerator

drawer

Name _____

Print the word for each object pictured

In the Kitchen 2

Name _____

Color each picture. Then, cut out the pictures and glue the ones that belong "In the Kitchen" in the boxes.

In the Kitchen

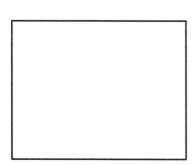
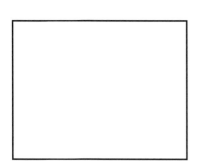

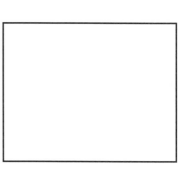

---

stove

refrigerator

cat

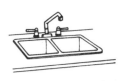

sink

dishwasher

microwave

drawer

bed

In the Kitchen 3

Name _____

Print each word.

kitchen

kitchen

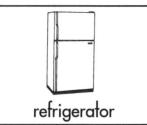
refrigerator

refrigerator

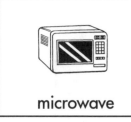
microwave

microwave

stove

stove

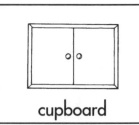
cupboard

cupboard

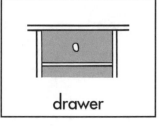
drawer

drawer

Name _____

Print each word.

 kitchen

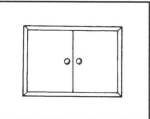 sink

 dishwasher

 stove

 cupboard

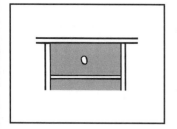 drawer

Cut out each picture and glue it by the correct word. Then, print each word.

	kitchen
	stove
	cupboard
	drawer
	dishwasher
	sink

Name _____

Cut out each picture and glue it by the correct word. Then, print each word.

refrigerator

drawer

microwave

sink

cupboard

stove

Name _____

Color the pictures to match the descriptions. Then, print the correct word under each picture.

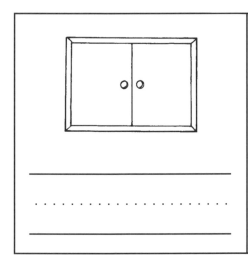

_____

. . . .

_____

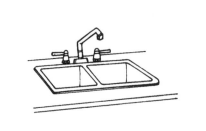

_____

. . . .

_____

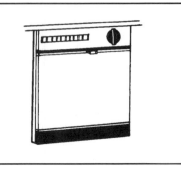

_____

. . . .

_____

1. The kitchen is green.
2. The drawer is brown.
3. The stove is yellow.
4. The cupboard is blue.
5. The dishwasher is red.
6. The sink is gray.

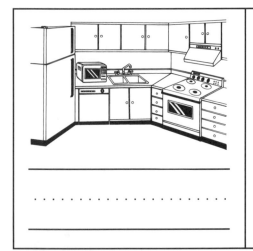

_____

. . . .

_____

_____

. . . .

_____

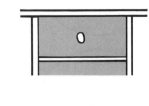

_____

. . . .

_____

Draw a picture for each sentence.

The stove is pink.

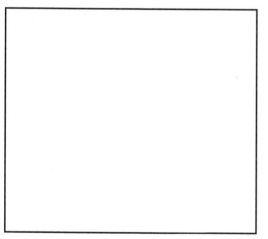

The cupboard is orange.

The sink is yellow.

Name _____

Draw a picture for each sentence.

The refrigerator is purple.

The microwave is green.

The drawer is black.

Complete each sentence.

Here is a ....

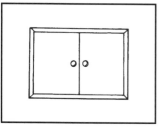

Here is a ....

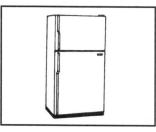

Here is a ....

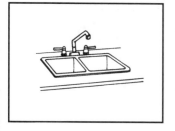

Here is a ....

Here is a ....

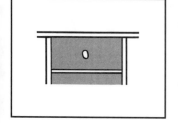

Here is a ....

In the Kitchen 8

Print the correct word under each picture.

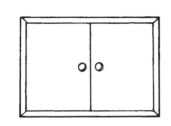

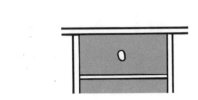

dishwasher

stove

kitchen

cupboard

sink

drawer

At the Table 1

Read the word for each object pictured.

glass

napkin

spoon

bowl

knife

mug

fork

plate

At the Table 1, cont.

Print the word for each object pictured.

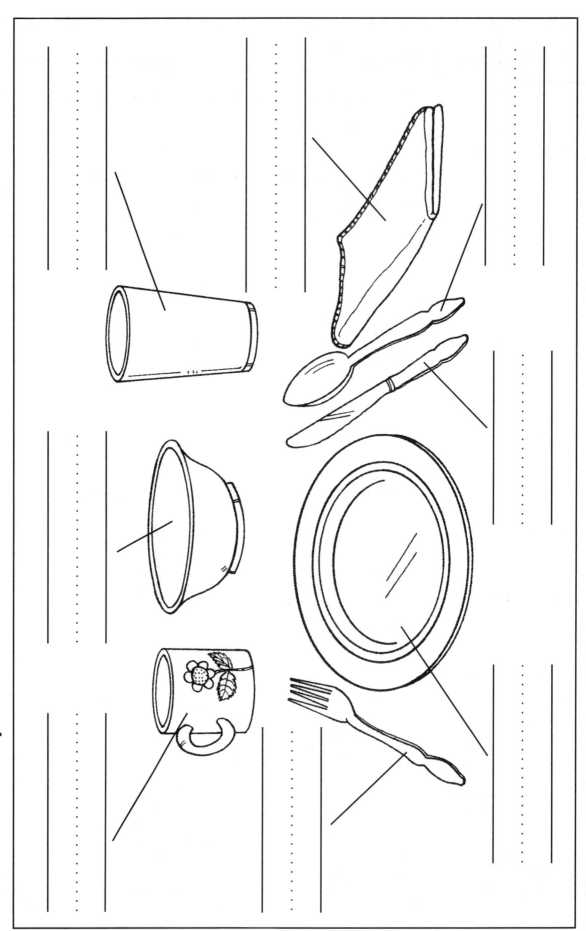

At the Table 2

Name _____

Print each word.

knife ·

fork ·

spoon ·

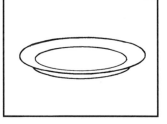

plate ·

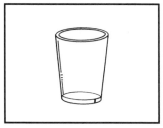

glass ·

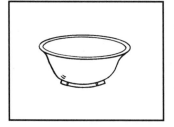

bowl ·

Name _____

Print each word.

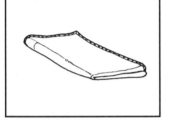

mug

napkin

kitchen

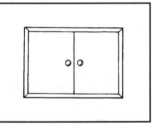

cupboard

drawer

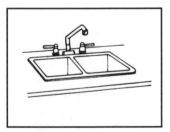

sink

At the Table 3

Name _____

Cut out each picture and glue it by the correct word. Then, print each word.

spoon _____

glass _____

plate _____

knife _____

fork _____

bowl _____

  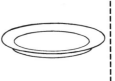

Cut out each picture and glue it by the correct word. Then, print each word.

	mug _____
	napkin _____
	cupboard _____
	drawer _____
	dishwasher _____
	sink _____

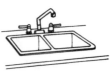
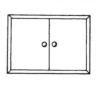

Print the correct word under each picture.

knife

fork   spoon

plate   glass

bowl

At the Table 5

Color the pictures to match the descriptions. Then, print the correct word under each picture.

1. The bowl is orange.
2. The mug is blue.
3. The glass is yellow.
4. The fork is gray.
5. The napkin is green.
6. The plate is pink.

At the Table 6

Draw a picture for each sentence.

I have a green glass.

I have a blue spoon.

I have a red plate.

Draw a picture for each sentence

I have a yellow mug.

I have a white napkin.

I have an orange fork.

At the Table 7

Name _____

Color the correct picture. Then, print the word.

napkin

plate

spoon

glass

Color the correct picture. Then, print the word.

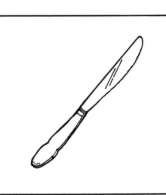 ⋯⋯⋯⋯⋯⋯⋯ knife ⋯⋯⋯⋯⋯⋯

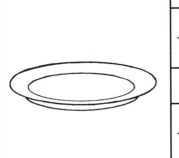 ⋯⋯⋯⋯⋯⋯⋯ fork ⋯⋯⋯⋯⋯⋯

 ⋯⋯⋯⋯⋯⋯⋯ mug ⋯⋯⋯⋯⋯⋯

 ⋯⋯⋯⋯⋯⋯⋯ bowl ⋯⋯⋯⋯⋯⋯

At the Table 8

Name _____

Circle the words on the right that are spelled correctly.

fork	fork korf	kfor fork	frok rofk	fork fork
spoon	spnoo spoon	spoon snoop	soonp spoon	spoon psoon
plate	palte plate	ptlae lptea	plate atepl	plate plate
mug	mug umg	gum gmu	mgu mug	mug mug
bowl	owlb wolb	lowb bowl	bowl lobw	bowl bowl
glass	glass algss	salgs glass	lagss glass	glass ssgla
napkin	npakin napkin	napink pinkan	napkin nikpan	napkin napkin

At the Table 9

Name _____

Answer each question with **yes** or **no**.

yes   no

1. Is this a knife?

2. Is this a spoon?

3. Is this a fork?

4. Is this a plate?

5. Is this a bowl?

6. Is this a glass?

7. Is this a napkin?

8. Is this a mug?

In the Living Room 1

Read the word for each object pictured.

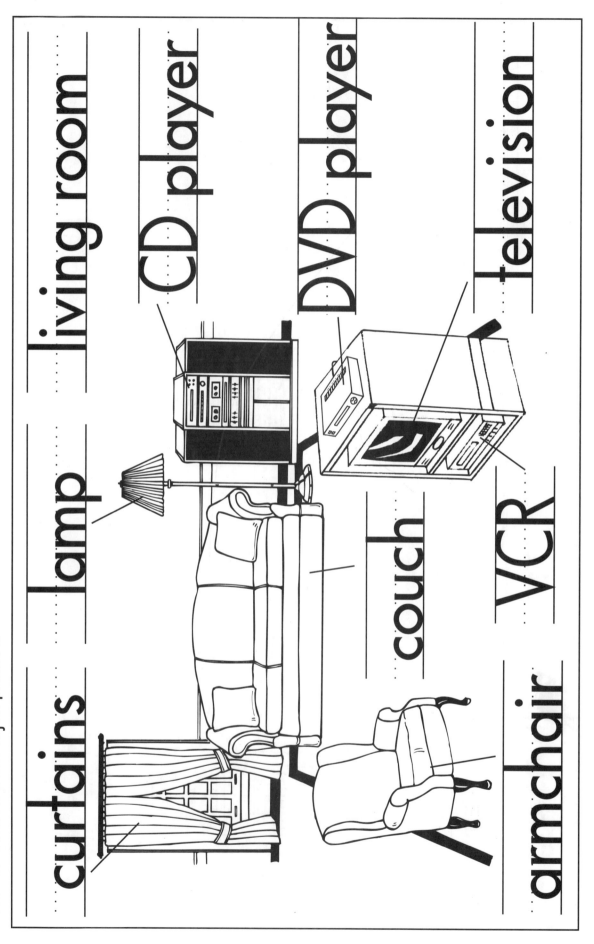

living room

CD player

DVD player

television

lamp

curtains

couch

VCR

armchair

In the Living Room 1, cont.

Name _____

Print the word for each object pictured.

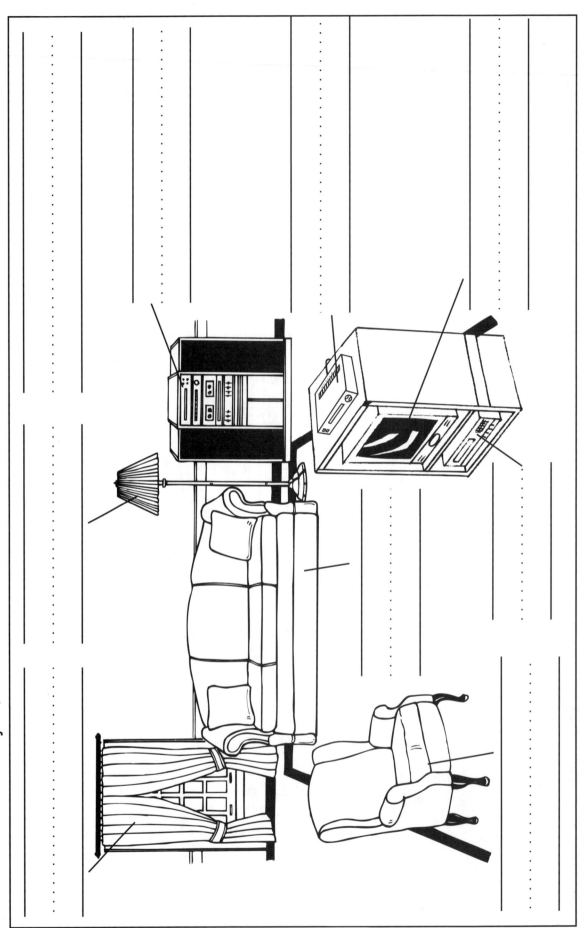

Name _____

Print each word.

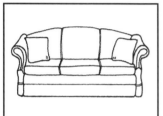 living room

 couch

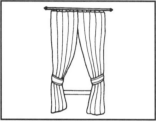 armchair

 curtains

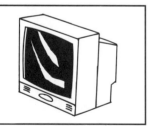 television

 lamp

Name _____

Print each word.

VCR

CD player

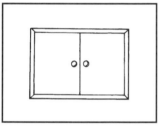

cupboard

glass

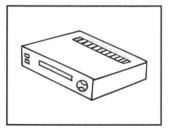

DVD player

In the Living Room 3

Name _____

Cut out each picture and glue it by the correct word. Then, print each word.

living room _____

couch _____

armchair _____

CD player _____

television _____

lamp _____

 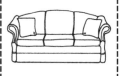

Name _____

Cut out each picture and glue it by the correct word. Then, print each word.

curtains

VCR

plate

bowl

DVD player

In the Living Room 4

Name _____

Color the pictures to match the descriptions. Then, print the correct word under each picture.

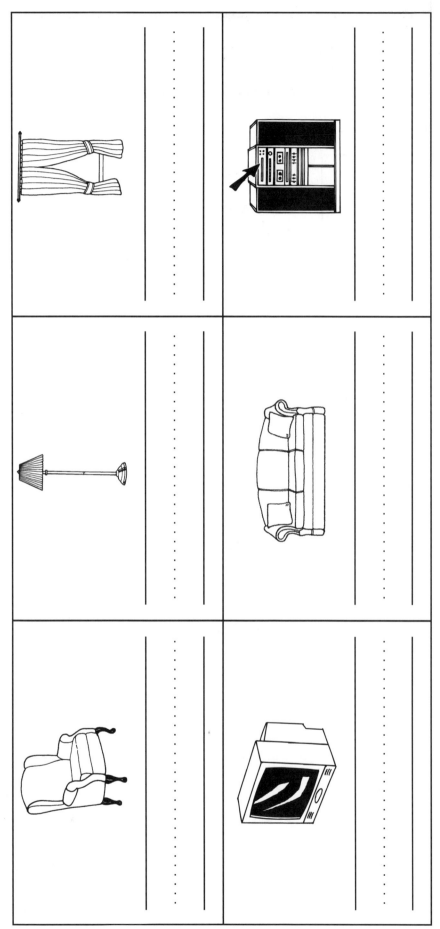

1. The couch is brown.
2. The curtains are green.
3. The CD player is blue.
4. The armchair is orange.
5. The television is yellow.
6. The lamp is white and purple.

Draw a picture for each sentence.

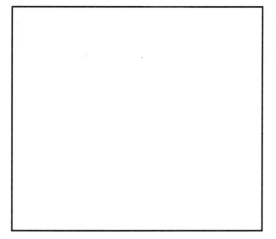

See the blue curtains.

See the brown television.

See the purple armchair.

Draw a picture for each sentence.

This is a couch.

This is a VCR.

This is a lamp.

In the Living Room 6

Name _____

Print the correct word under each picture.

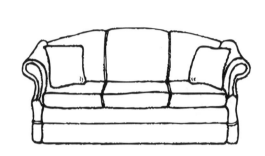

_____

_____

_____

living room

curtains   lamp

VCR   couch

armchair

_____

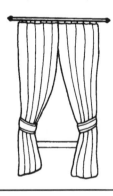

_____

_____

Print the correct word under each picture.

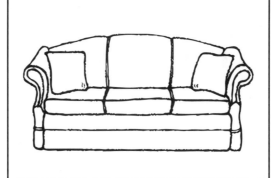

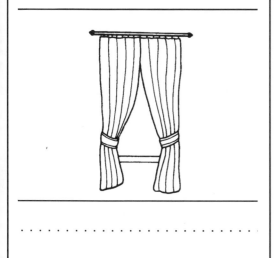

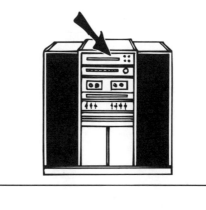

couch

armchair

curtains

CD player

television

lamp

Name _____

Complete each sentence.

 This is a _____ .

 This is an _____ .

 This is a _____ .

 This is a _____ .

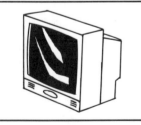 This is a _____ .

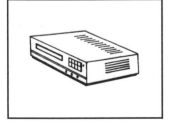 This is a _____ .

Complete each sentence.

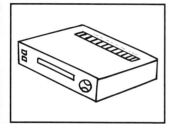 This is a ....

 This is a ....

....

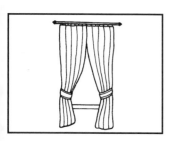 These are ....

 This is a ....

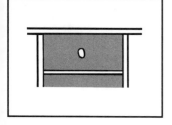 This is a ....

Read the word for each object pictured.

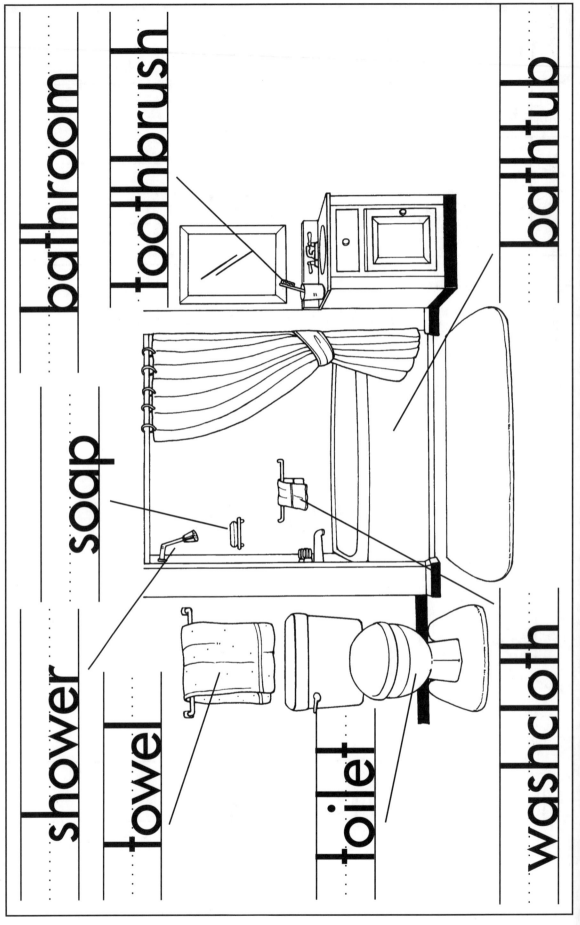

bathroom

toothbrush

bathtub

soap

shower

towel

toilet

washcloth

In the Bathroom 1, cont.

Name _____

Print the word for each object pictured.

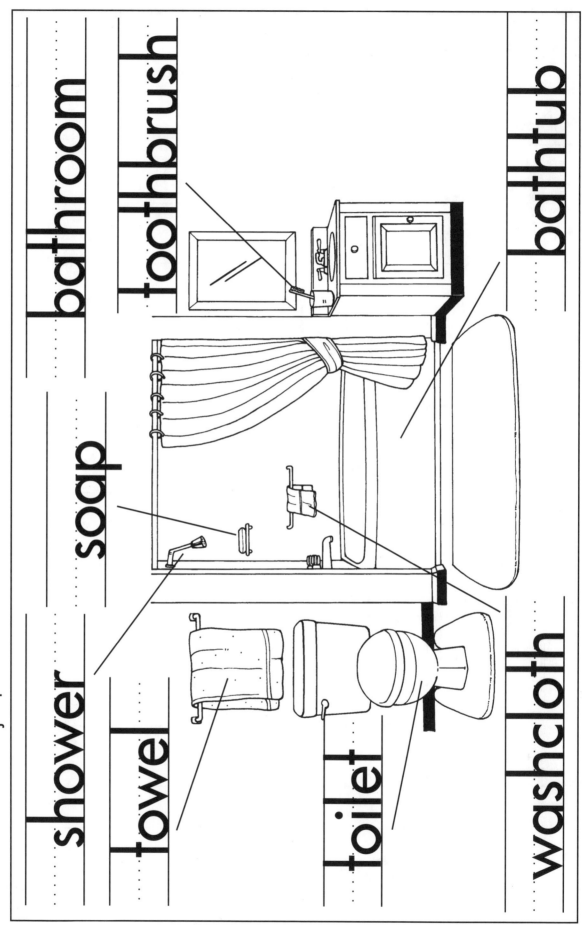

bathroom

toothbrush

bathtub

soap

shower

towel

toilet

washcloth

In the Bathroom 2

Name _____

Print each word.

 **bathroom**

 **toilet**

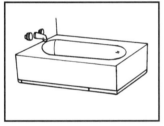 **bathtub**

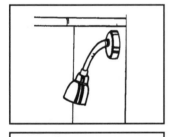 **shower**

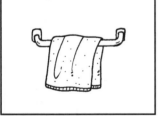 **washcloth**

 **towel**

Print each word.

soap

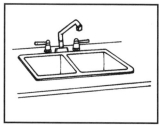

toothbrush

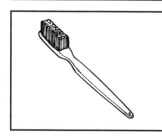

sink

glass

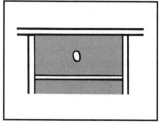

drawer

lamp

In the Bathroom 3

Name _____

Cut out each picture and glue it by the correct word. Then, print each word.

<u>bathroom</u> ....

<u>toilet</u> ....

<u>bathtub</u> ....

<u>shower</u> ....

<u>towel</u> ....

<u>soap</u> ....

Cut out each picture and glue it by the correct word. Then, print each word.

washcloth

sink

toothbrush

drawer

cupboard

glass

  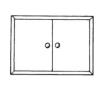   

In the Bathroom 4

Print the correct word under each picture.

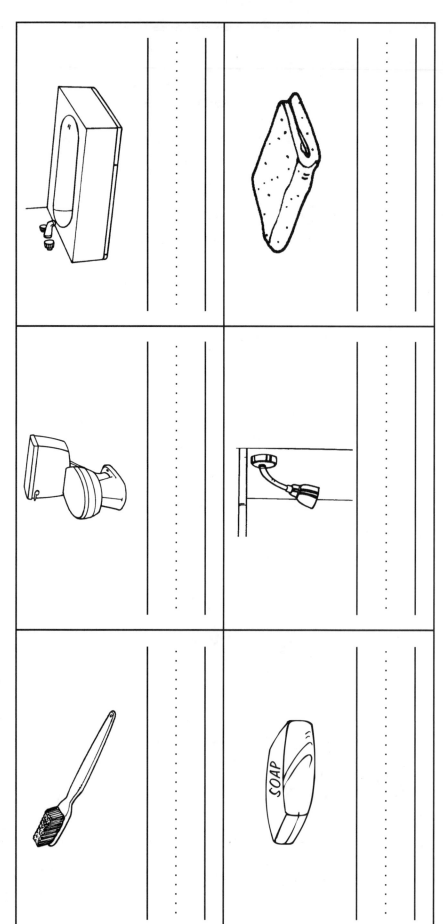

towel

soap

toothbrush

toilet

bathtub

shower

Complete each sentence.

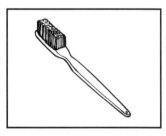 I see the _____.

 I see the _____.

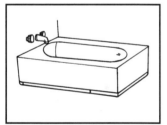 I see the _____.

 I see the _____.

 I see the _____.

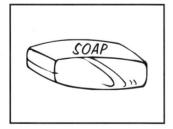 I see the _____.

In the Bathroom 6

Name _____

Color the correct picture. Then, print the word.

 bathroom

 bathtub

 shower

 toilet

Color the correct picture. Then, print the word.

washcloth

towel

soap

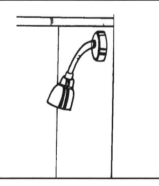

toothbrush

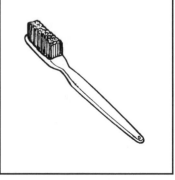

In the Bathroom 7

Name _____

Complete each sentence with **in** or **out**.

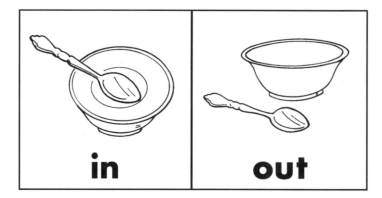

in   out

The soap is _____ of the sink.

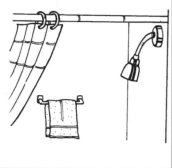

The washcloth is _____ the shower.

The toothbrush is _____ the bathroom.

Complete each sentence with **in** or **out**.

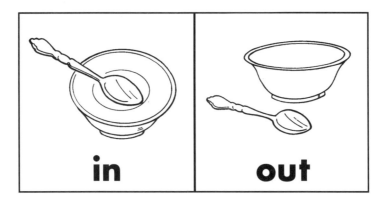

The glass is _____ ....
of the cupboard.

The towel is _____ ....
of the bathtub.

The armchair is _____ ....
the living room.

In the Bathroom 8

Name _____

Print each word where it belongs.

In the Bathroom	**In the Living Room**

couch   television   armchair   curtains   toothbrush

shower   toilet   bathtub   washcloth   VCR

CD player   soap   towel   lamp

Read the word for each object pictured.

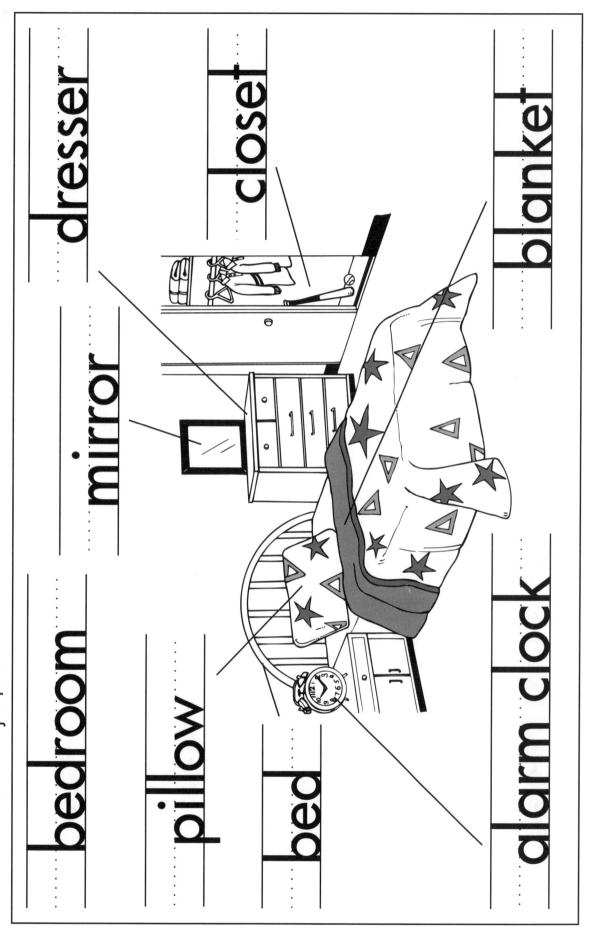

dresser

closet

blanket

mirror

bedroom

pillow

bed

alarm clock

In the Bedroom 1, cont.

Print the word for each object pictured.

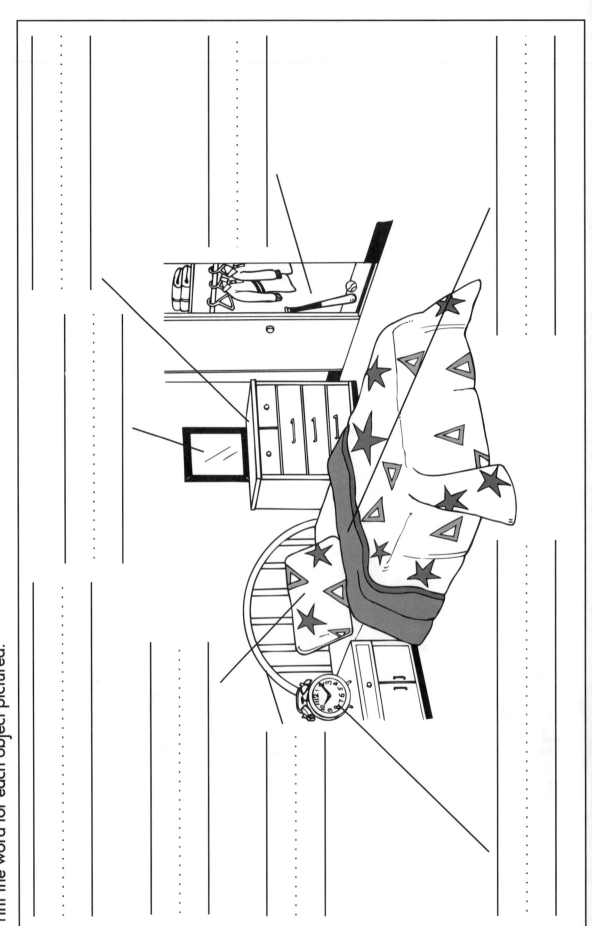

In the Bedroom 2

Name _____

Print each word.

 **bedroom**

 **bed**

 **dresser**

mirror

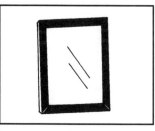 **closet**

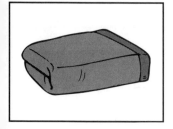 **blanket**

Name _____

Print each word.

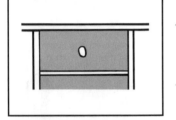 pillow

 alarm clock

 lamp

 drawer

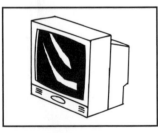 television

 glass

In the Bedroom 3

Name _____

Cut out each picture and glue it by the correct word. Then, print each word.

bedroom

dresser

mirror

bed

blanket

pillow

Name _____

Cut out each picture and glue it by the correct word. Then, print each word.

<u>alarm clock</u>

<u>closet</u>

<u>armchair</u>

<u>lamp</u>

<u>television</u>

<u>curtains</u>

   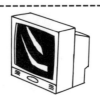 

Name _____

Print the correct word under each picture.

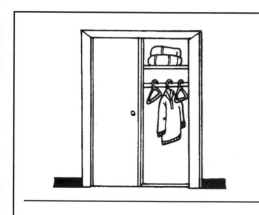

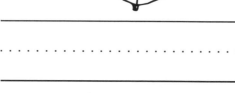

blanket

pillow

bed

dresser

closet

mirror

Complete each sentence.

 I have a _____ .

 I have a _____ .

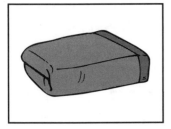 I have a _____ .

 I have a _____ .

 I have a _____ .

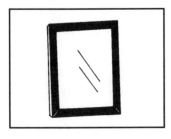 I have a _____ .

Complete each sentence.

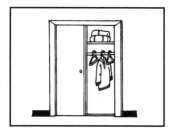 I have a _____ .

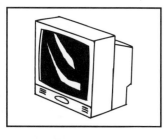 I have an _____
_____ .

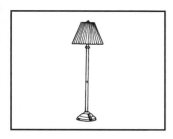 I have a _____ .

 I have a _____ .

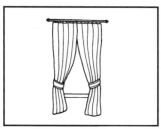 I have _____ .

In the Bedroom 7

Name _____

Complete each sentence with **near** or **far**.

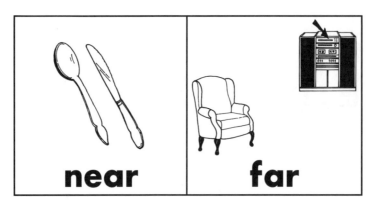

near   **far**

The towel is _____ the alarm clock.

The mirror is _____ the washcloth.

The dresser is _____ from the lamp.

Complete each sentence with **near** or **far**.

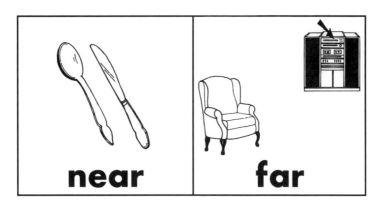

near   **far**

A lamp is _____
the bed.

The television is _____
the blanket.

The fork is _____
from the closet.

Name _____

Complete each sentence with **near** or **far**.

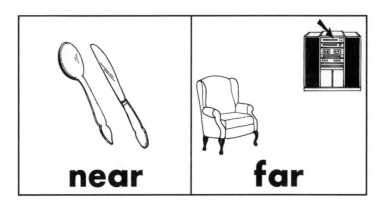

near   **far**

The pillow is _____
from the alarm clock.

The bed is _____
the sink.

The dresser is _____
the curtains.

In the Bedroom 8

Name _____

Print each word where it belongs.

In the Living Room	In the Bedroom
_____	_____
_____	_____
_____	_____
_____	_____
_____	_____
_____	_____

bed   blanket   CD player   VCR

couch   television   dresser   curtains

armchair   pillow   closet   alarm clock

In the Bedroom 9

Name _____

Complete each sentence.

1. The bathtub is in the _____
   (living room   bathroom) _____

2. The stove is in the _____
   (kitchen   bedroom) _____

3. The soap is in the _____
   (refrigerator   bathroom) _____

4. The bed is in the _____
   (bedroom   kitchen) _____

5. The shower is in the _____
   (bedroom   bathroom) _____

6. The spoon is in the _____
   (bowl   fork) _____

7. The sink is in the _____
   (kitchen   living room) _____

8. The plate is in the _____
   (bathtub   dishwasher) _____

9. The mug is in the _____
   (cupboard   shower) _____

10. The dresser is in the _____
    (kitchen   bedroom) _____

Vocabulary List

Part 1

alarm clock	drawer	plate
armchair	dresser	refrigerator
bathroom	DVD player	shower
bathtub	fork	sink
bed	glass	soap
bedroom	kitchen	spoon
blanket	knife	stove
bowl	lamp	television
CD player	living room	toilet
closet	microwave	toothbrush
couch	mirror	towel
cupboard	mug	VCR
curtains	napkin	washcloth
dishwasher	pillow	

Name: _____

Read the word for each object pictured.

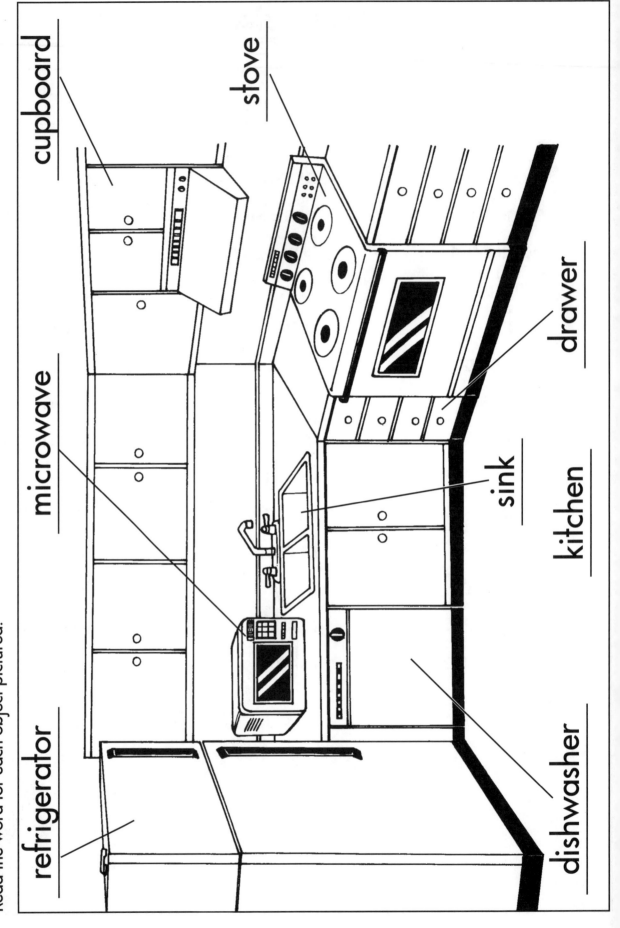

cupboard

stove

microwave

refrigerator

drawer

sink

kitchen

dishwasher

Name:

Write the word for each object pictured.

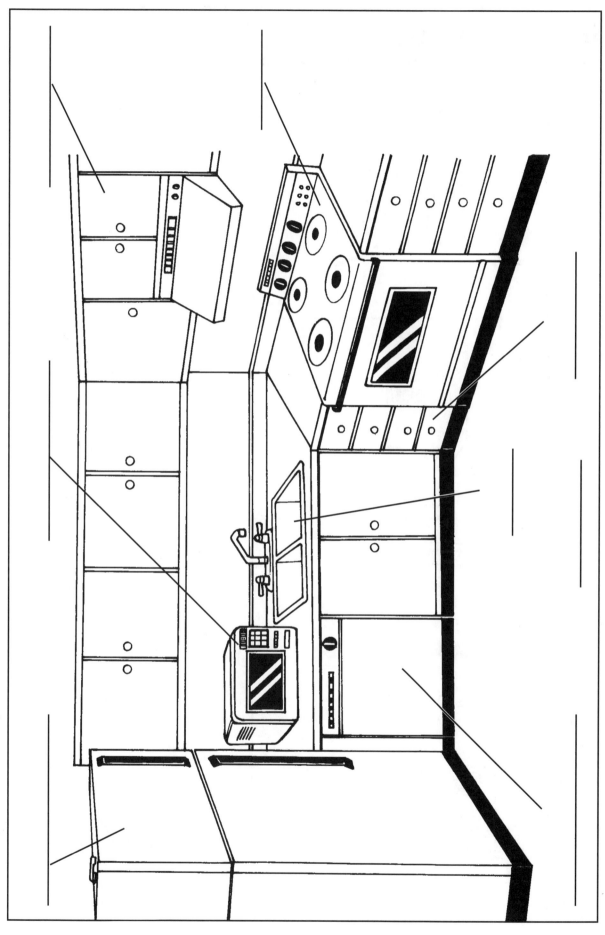

In the Kitchen 2

Here are some words for you to use.

kitchen	refrigerator
stove	microwave
dishwasher	cupboard
sink	drawer

In the Kitchen 2, cont.

Write the word for each object.

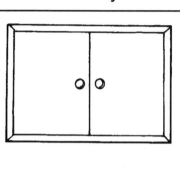

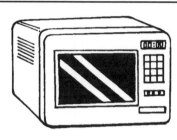

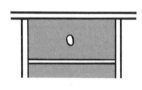

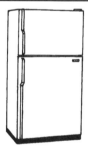

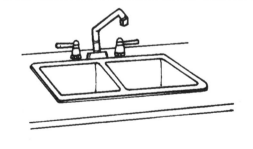

Color the pictures to match the descriptions. Then, write the correct word under each picture.

1. The kitchen is green.

2. The drawer is brown.

3. The stove is yellow.

4. The cupboard is blue.

5. The dishwasher is red.

6. The sink is gray.

Name:

Complete each sentence.

Here is a _____.

Here is a _____.

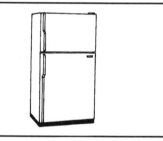

Here is a _____.

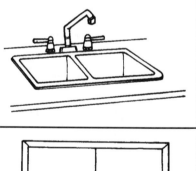

Here is a _____.

Here is a _____.

Here is a _____.

In the Kitchen 5

Name: _____

Mark **true** or **false** for each statement.

1. We can pull out a drawer.   __true   __false

2. Sometimes there are nice smells in the kitchen.   __true   __false

3. We wash our dishes in the microwave.   __true   __false

4. A stove can get very hot.   __true   __false

5. A sink has a drain and a faucet.   __true   __false

6. We cook our dinner on the refrigerator.   __true   __false

7. Most cupboards have doors you can open and close.   __true   __false

8. Lots of people can sit in the dishwasher.   __true   __false

In the Kitchen 6

Name:

Fill in the blank.

1. He cooks a pot of stew on the _____.

2. The _____ washes dishes.

3. The faucet is dripping water into the _____.

4. Pull out the _____ and put away the clean spoons.

5. Mom said, "Put the dishes on the top shelf of the

    _____."

6. She warms her lunch in the _____.

7. The _____ keeps our milk cold.

8. You can cook and store food in the _____.

drawer   dishwasher

kitchen   refrigerator

stove   sink

microwave   cupboard

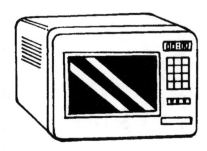

At the Table 1

Read the word for each object pictured.

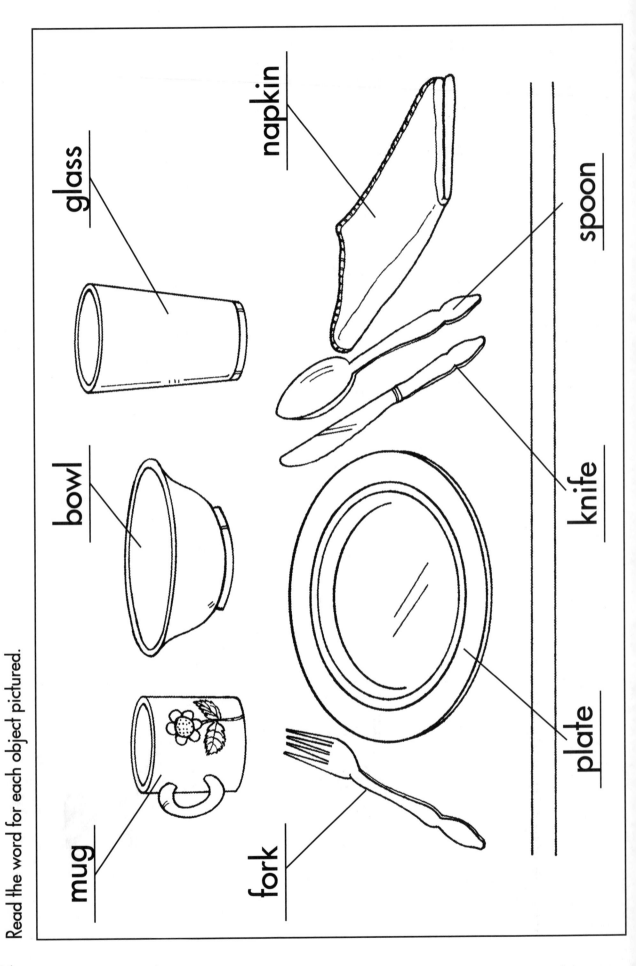

glass

napkin

spoon

bowl

knife

mug

plate

fork

At the Table 1, cont.

Write the word for each object pictured.

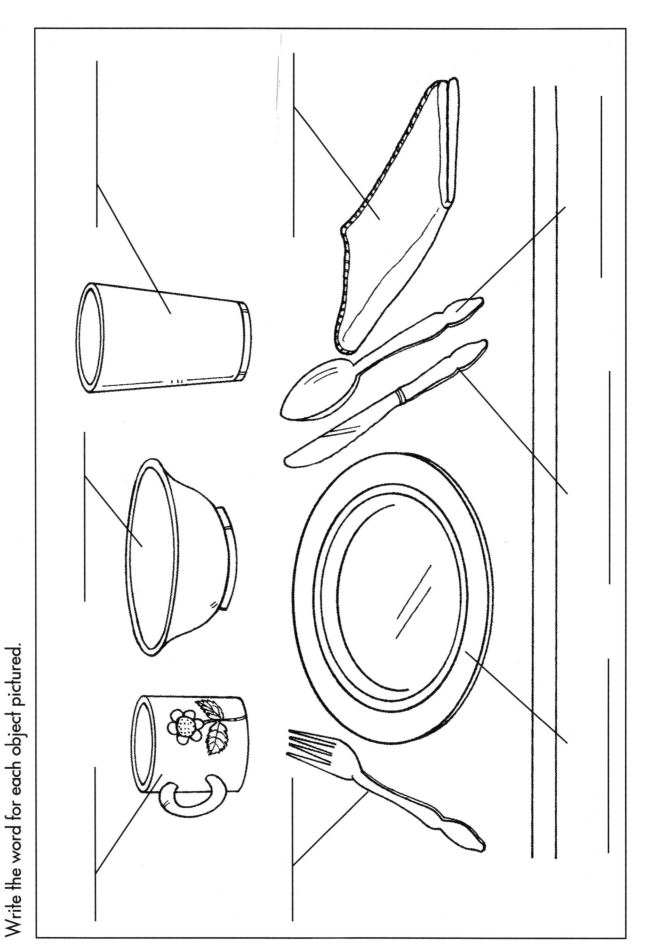

At the Table 2

Here are some words for you to use.

knife	fork
spoon	plate
bowl	mug
glass	napkin

Write the word for each object.

At the Table 3

Color the pictures to match the descriptions. Then, write each word under the correct picture.

1. The bowl is orange.

2. The mug is blue.

3. The glass is yellow.

4. The fork is gray.

5. The napkin is green.

6. The plate is pink.

Level 2, Part 1
Basic Vocabulary – Home

104

At the Table 4

Name: _____

Answer each question with **yes** or **no**.

yes   no

1. Is this a knife?   _____

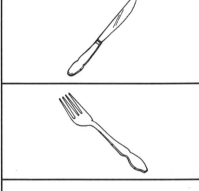

2. Is this a spoon?   _____

3. Is this a fork?   _____

4. Is this a plate?   _____

5. Is this a bowl?   _____

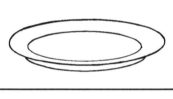

6. Is this a glass?   _____

7. Is this a napkin?   _____

8. Is this a mug?   _____

At the Table 5

Mark **true** or **false** for each statement.

1. A glass is easy to break.   __true   __false

2. A bowl has four legs and a tail.   __true   __false

3. A knife can be very dangerous.   __true   __false

4. We drive a plate to school.   __true   __false

5. A spoon is always flat.   __true   __false

6. We might put a napkin on our lap.   __true   __false

7. A fork helps us jump over the table.   __true   __false

8. We can put hot drinks in a mug.   __true   __false

_____
_____

At the Table 6

Name: _____

Fill in the blank.

1. I fill my _____ with hot vegetable soup.

2. The _____ is very sharp.

3. Hot coffee tastes good from a _____ .

4. Mother gave me a cold _____ of milk.

5. You eat soup with a _____ .

6. She eats her salad with a _____ .

7. I wipe my mouth with a _____ .

8. There are vegetables and meat on my _____ .

mug	fork
bowl	napkin
knife	spoon
plate	glass

In the Living Room 1

Name: _____

Read the word for each object pictured.

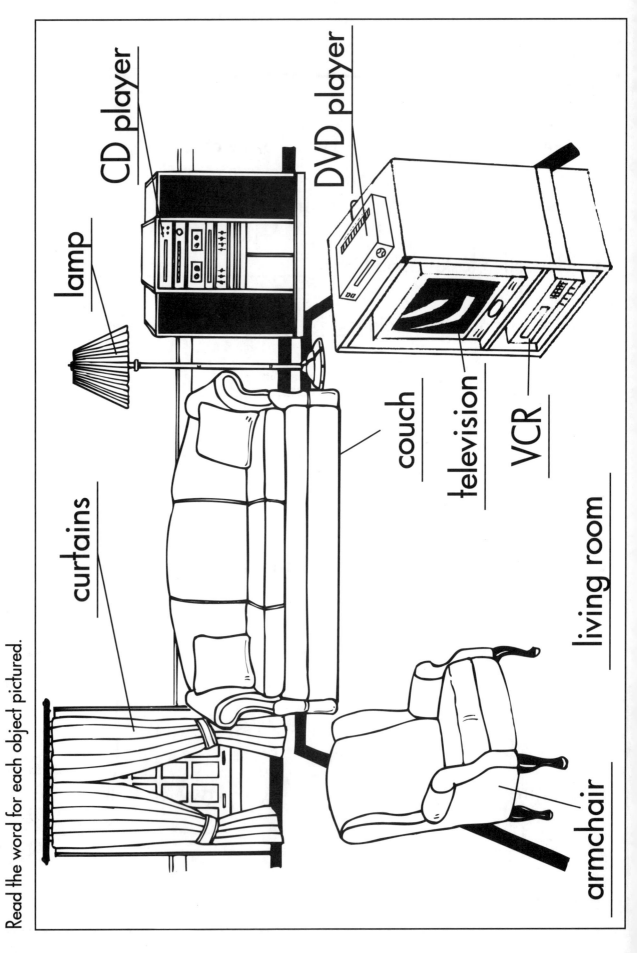

CD player

DVD player

lamp

curtains

couch

television

VCR

living room

armchair

In the Living Room 1, cont.

Write the word for each object pictured.

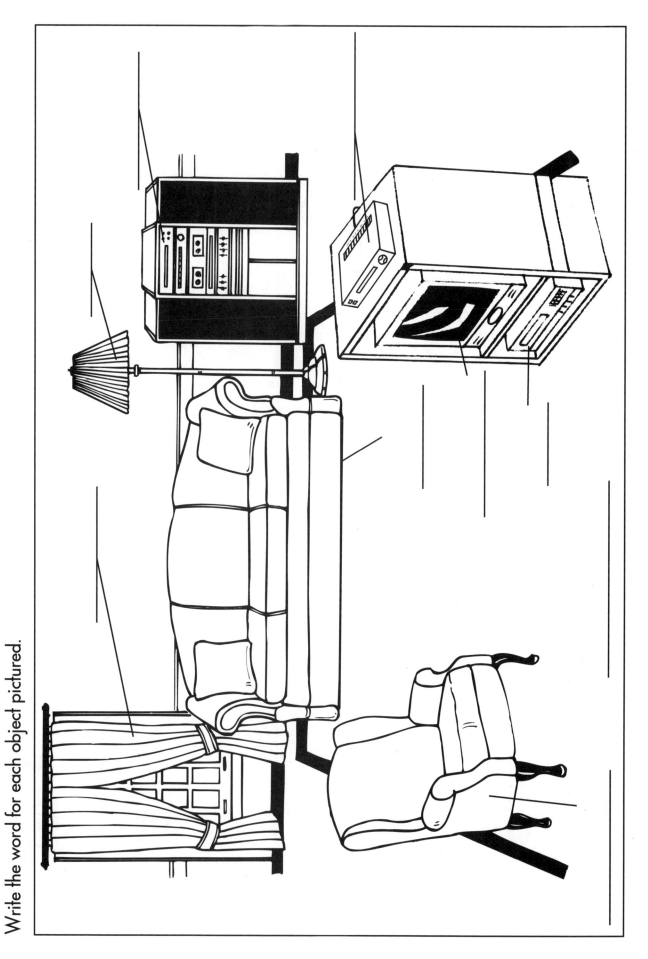

Name:

Here are some words for you to use.

couch

armchair

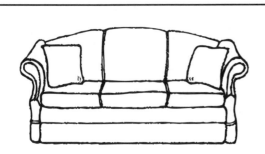

living room

curtains

CD player

television

lamp

VCR

In the Living Room 2, cont.

Write the word for each object.

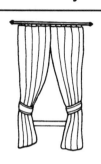

_____

_____

_____

_____

_____

_____

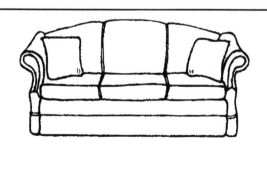

_____

_____

Level 2, Part 1
Basic Vocabulary – Home

111

In the Living Room 3

Name:

Color the pictures to match the descriptions. Then, write each word under the correct picture.

1. The couch is brown.

2. The curtains are green.

3. The CD player is blue.

4. The armchair is orange.

5. The television is yellow.

6. The lamp is white and purple.

In the Living Room 4

Write the correct word under each picture.

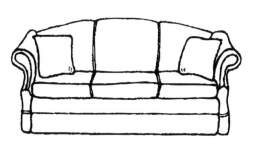

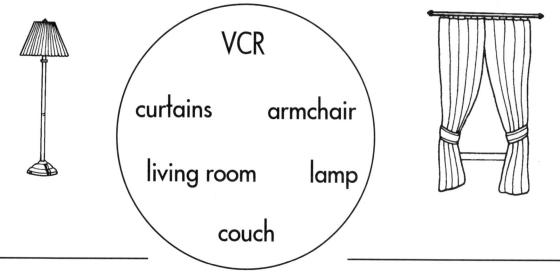

VCR

curtains   armchair

living room   lamp

couch

In the Living Room 5

Name:

Complete each sentence.

This is a _____.

This is an _____.

This is a _____.

This is a _____.

This is a _____.

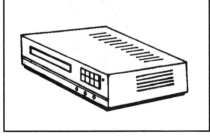

This is a _____.

In the Living Room 5, cont.

Complete each sentence.

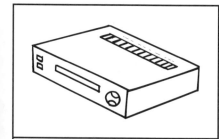

This is a _____ .

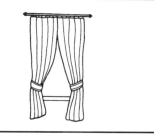

This is a _____ .

These are _____ .

This is a _____ .

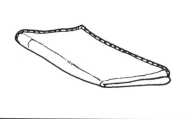

This is a _____ .

This is a _____ .

In the Living Room 6

Name:

Mark **true** or **false** for each statement.

1. Curtains can help to make a room dark.   __true   __false

2. A lamp should have a light bulb.   __true   __false

3. We can watch the news on television.   __true   __false

4. An armchair might be a comfortable place to sit and read.   __true   __false

5. A living room can have furniture in it.   __true   __false

6. We can clean a room with a VCR.   __true   __false

7. We watch cartoons on the CD player.   __true   __false

8. A couch should be put in the dishwasher.   __true   __false

Fill in the blank.

1. Our family watches television in the _____ .

2. There is room for only me to sit in my favorite
   _____ .

3. Open the _____ if you want more sunlight.

4. My dad, sister, and I sit on the _____ .

5. I listen to music on the _____ .

6. Turn on the _____ to read your book.

7. We rent a movie and put it in the _____
   to watch it.

8. What is your favorite show on _____ ?

DVD player
armchair
lamp
television
living room
couch
curtains
CD player

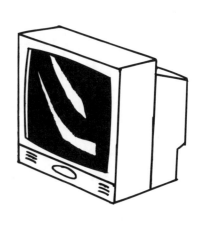

In the Bathroom 1

Read the word for each object pictured.

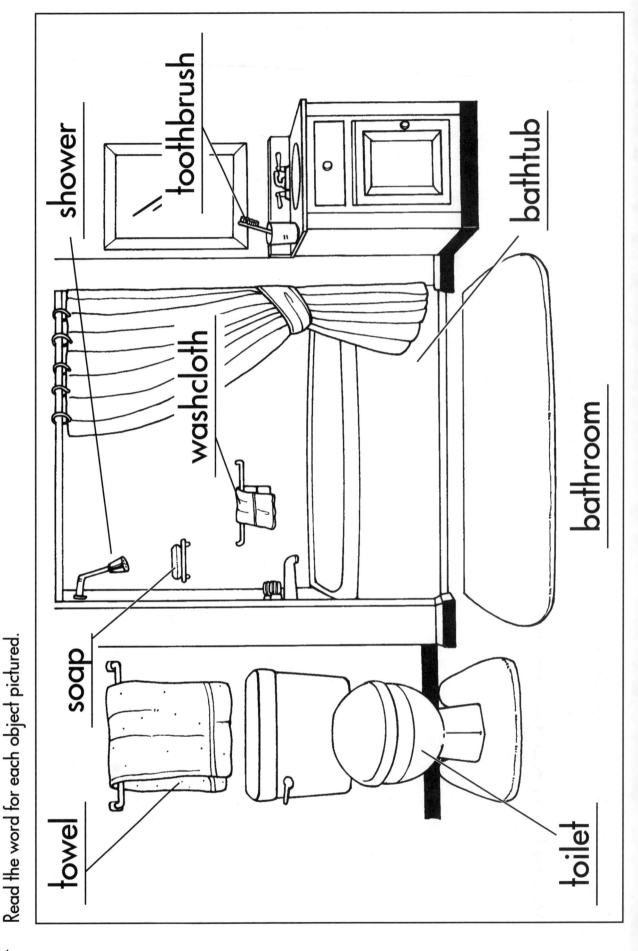

shower

toothbrush

bathtub

washcloth

bathroom

soap

towel

toilet

In the Bathroom 1, cont.

Write the word for each object pictured.

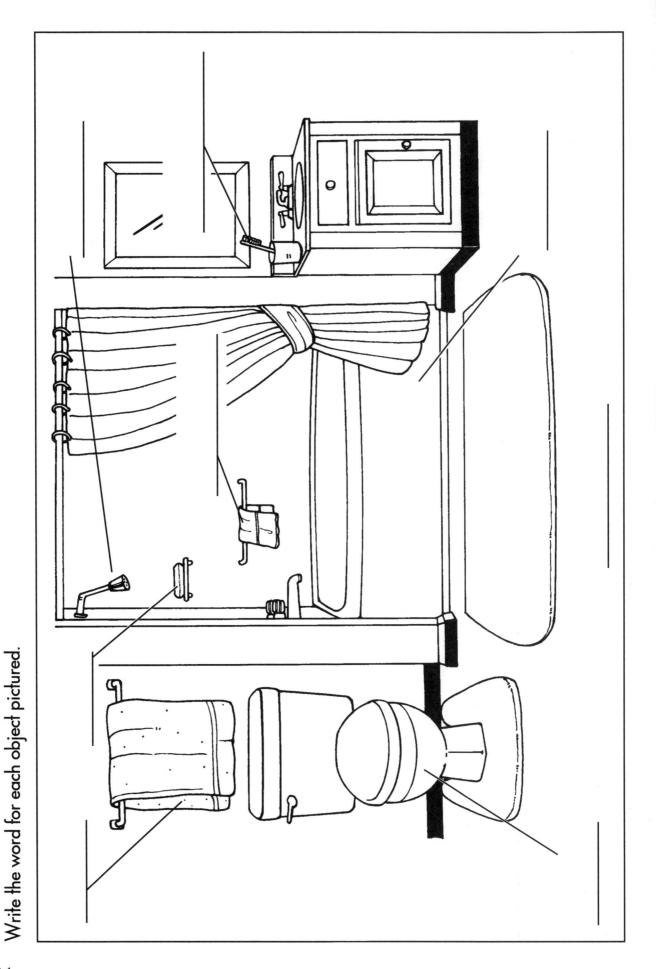

In the Bathroom 2

Name:

Here are some words for you to use.

bathroom

toilet

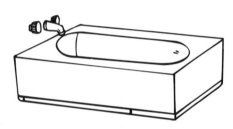

bathtub

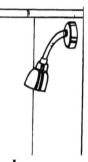

shower

towel

soap

washcloth

toothbrush

In the Bathroom 2, cont.

Write the word for each object.

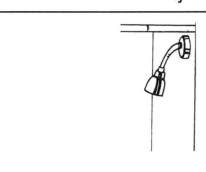

_____

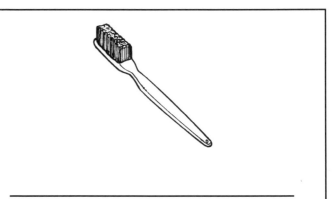

_____

_____

_____

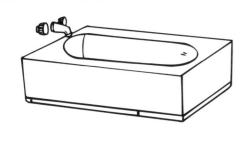

_____

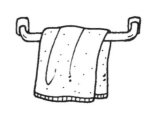

_____

_____

_____

In the Bathroom 3

Name: _____

Complete each sentence.

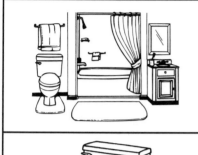

I see the _____.

I see the _____.

I see the _____.

I see the _____.

I see the _____.

I see the _____.

In the Bathroom 4

Name: _____

Complete each sentence with **in** or **out**.

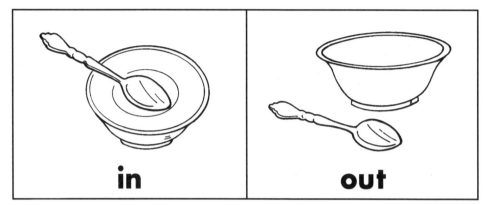

in   out

The soap is _____ of the sink.

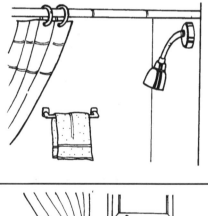

The washcloth is _____ the shower.

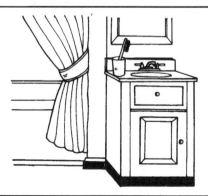

The toothbrush is _____ the bathroom.

Complete each sentence with **in** or **out**.

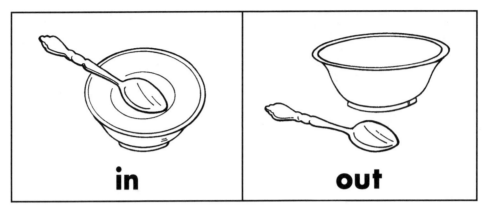

in   out

The glass is _____ of
the cupboard.

The towel is _____ of
the bathtub.

The armchair is _____
the living room.

In the Bathroom 5

Write each word in the correct column.

In the Living Room

_____

_____

_____

_____

_____

_____

In the Bathroom

_____

_____

_____

_____

_____

_____

couch   shower

CD player   television

toilet   soap

armchair   bathtub

towel   curtains

washcloth   lamp

toothbrush   VCR

In the Bathroom 6

Name:

Mark **true** or **false** for each statement.

1. Towels come in many colors. __true __false

2. You use soap to wash your hands. __true __false

3. You can cut your meat with a toothbrush. __true __false

4. A washcloth has two eyes, a nose, and a mouth. __true __false

5. You usually find a toilet in the bathroom. __true __false

6. A bathtub tells you the time. __true __false

7. You might take a bath in the bathtub. __true __false

8. You write letters in the shower. __true __false

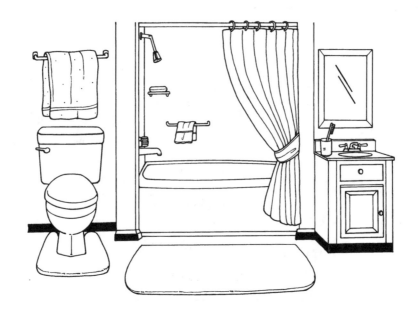

In the Bathroom 7

Name:

Fill in the blank.

1. The _____ is a good place to brush your teeth.

2. You use a _____ to wash your face.

3. I dry myself with a _____ .

4. Flush the _____ .

5. He stands under the _____ to wash his hair.

6. The bar of _____ slips out of my hand.

7. I fill the _____ with warm water before
   I take a bath.

8. She put the toothpaste on her _____ .

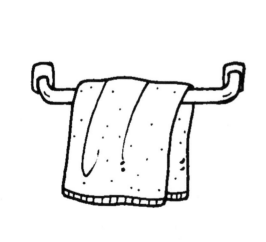

towel
toilet
bathroom
soap
bathtub
washcloth
toothbrush
shower

In the Bedroom 1

Name:

Read the word for each object pictured.

mirror

alarm clock

closet

dresser

bed

pillow

blanket

bedroom

In the Bedroom 1, cont.

Name: _____

Write the word for each object pictured.

In the Bedroom 2

Here are some words for you to use.

bedroom	bed

closet	dresser

blanket	mirror

alarm clock	pillow

Name:

Write the word for each object.

_____

_____

_____

_____

_____

_____

_____

_____

Level 2, Part 1
Basic Vocabulary – Home

131

In the Bedroom 3

Name:

Complete each sentence with **near** or **far**.

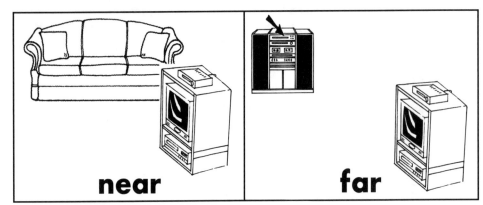

near   **far**

The towel is _____ the alarm clock.

The mirror is _____ the washcloth.

The dresser is _____ from the lamp.

Complete each sentence with **near** or **far**.

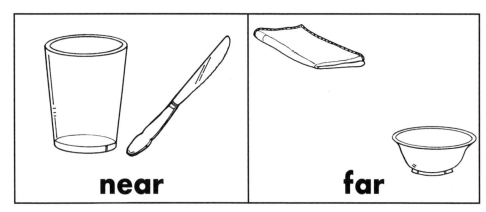

near   **far**

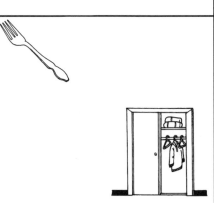
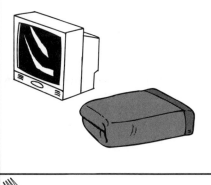

The lamp is _____ the bed.

The television is _____ the blanket.

The fork is _____ from the closet.

Complete each sentence with **near** or **far**.

near   far

The pillow is _____ from the alarm clock.

The bed is _____ the sink.

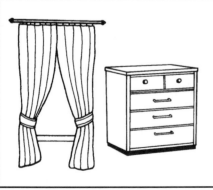

The dresser is _____ the curtains.

In the Bedroom 4

Name:

Write each word in the correct column.

In the Living Room

_____

_____

_____

_____

_____

_____

In the Bedroom

_____

_____

_____

_____

_____

_____

bed
blanket
armchair
dresser
DVD player
alarm clock

CD player
television
pillow
curtains
closet

In the Bedroom 5

Name:

Complete each sentence.

1. The bathtub is in the

    _____ .

    (living room   bathroom)

2. The stove is in the

    _____ .

    (kitchen   bedroom)

3. The soap is in the

    _____ .

    (refrigerator   bathroom)

4. The bed is in the

    _____ .

    (bedroom   kitchen)

5. The shower is in the

    _____ .

    (bedroom   bathroom)

6. The spoon is in the

    _____ .

    (bowl   fork)

7. The sink is in the

    _____ .

    (kitchen   living room)

8. The plate is in the

    _____ .

    (bathtub   dishwasher)

9. The mug is in the

    _____ .

    (cupboard   shower)

10. The dresser is in the

    _____ .

    (kitchen   bedroom)

Mark **true** or **false** for each statement.

1. You can make funny faces in a mirror.   __true   __false

2. A bed has arms.   __true   __false

3. A closet can have a door that opens and closes.   __true   __false

4. Some people sleep in a bedroom.   __true   __false

5. A pillow can be soft and comfortable.   __true   __false

6. A dresser is where we keep our food.   __true   __false

7. A blanket can be made of wool.   __true   __false

8. You use an alarm clock to brush your hair.   __true   __false

In the Bedroom 7

Name:

Fill in the blank.

1. I see myself in the _____ .

2. I need another _____ to keep me warm.

3. The _____ wakes me up in the morning.

4. Hang your shirts in the _____ .

5. Those socks go in your _____ .

6. Make your _____ in the morning.

7. The movers put the bed and dresser in the _____ .

8. A pillow case goes on a _____ .

alarm clock   closet

bed   mirror

blanket   bedroom

pillow   dresser

Vocabulary List

Part 2

appliances	door bell	laundry room
attic	driveway	oven
balcony	dryer	patio
basement	elevator	porch
blender	end table	radio
carport	fireplace	roof
chimney	furnace	swimming pool
china cabinet	furniture	toaster
closet	freezer	toys
coffee table	garage	vacuum
crib	garden	wall unit
dining room	hall	washer

Following Directions 1

Read each direction and see how it's used.

draw	dresser
color	
write	fork <u>fork</u>
fill in the blanks	The <u>stove</u> is <u>hot</u> .
cross out	knife fork sh~~o~~wer spoon
underline	knife fork <u>shower</u> spoon
circle	knife fork (shower) spoon
copy	CD player <u>CD player</u>
match	couch carpet carpet napkin napkin couch
label	knife fork plate

Follow each direction.

color	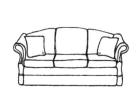 
cross out	refrigerator stove dishwasher bed
circle	washcloth soap armchair towel
draw	lamp
fill in the blank	napkin VCR I wipe my face with a _____.
copy	alarm clock _____

Follow each direction.

write	microwave _____
underline	pillow sink bed blanket
fill in the blank	bathtub plate The _____ is on the table.
match	kitchen bathroom bedroom bedroom bathroom kitchen
cross out	plate bowl mug shower
label	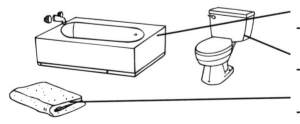 _____ _____ _____

Following Directions 2

Name:

Follow the directions to complete the picture.

draw: a pillow, a blanket, a mirror, an alarm clock

write: your name on the sign on the wall

cross out: the mirror

circle: the alarm clock

underline: your name

label: the bed, the pillow, and the blanket

color: the picture

'S ROOM

Places at Home 1

Name:

Here are some words for you to use.

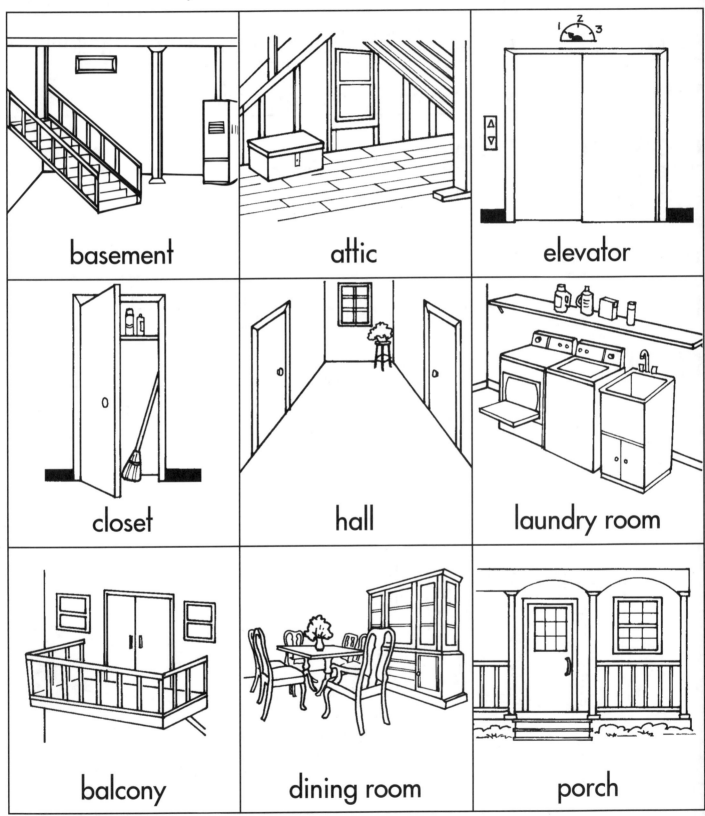

basement

attic

elevator

closet

hall

laundry room

balcony

dining room

porch

Places at Home 2

Copy each word twice.

basement   _____   _____

attic   _____   _____

elevator   _____   _____

closet   _____   _____

hall   _____   _____

laundry room   _____   _____

balcony   _____   _____

dining room   _____   _____

porch   _____   _____

Places at Home 3

Complete each sentence with a phrase from the box. Then, write the sentence.

The sink is _____

_____

The man is _____

_____

The refrigerator is _____

_____

The woman is _____

_____

The bird is _____

_____

The elevator is _____

_____

out of the elevator	in the basement
near the porch	far from the balcony
in the hall	by the closet

Places at Home 4

Fill in the blank.

1. The part of a building that is underground is called a

    _____ .

2. I sit on the _____ outside my apartment.

3. The _____ door closes and we go up to the
    fifth floor.

4. There are many washers and dryers in the _____

    _____ .

5. When I get out of the elevator, I walk down the _____
    to my apartment.

6. This tall _____ holds a mop and a broom.

7. I sit on the _____ outside my house.

8. Many people can eat at the table in our _____

    _____ .

balcony	porch	dining room
basement	laundry room	attic
elevator	closet	hall

Outside the Home 1

Here are some words for you to use.

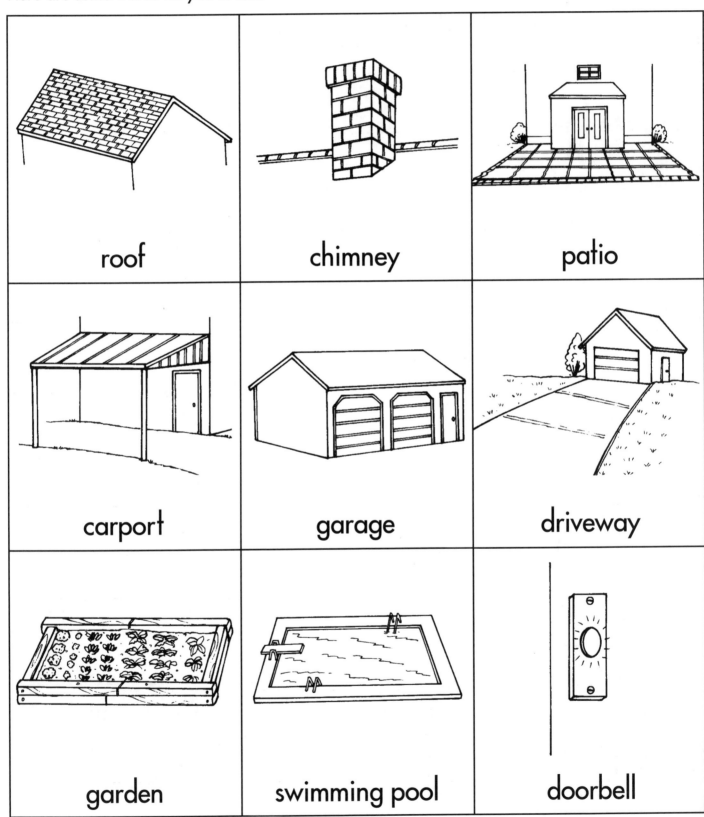

roof	chimney	patio
carport	garage	driveway
garden	swimming pool	doorbell

Outside the Home 2

Copy each word twice.

roof _____ _____

chimney _____ _____

patio _____ _____

carport _____ _____

garage _____ _____

driveway _____ _____

garden _____ _____

swimming pool _____ _____

doorbell _____ _____

Outside the Home 3

Draw pictures for eight of the words in the box. Label each picture.

roof	chimney	patio
carport	garage	driveway
garden	swimming pool	doorbell

Outside the Home 4

Name: _____

Write a sentence for each picture.

_____

_____

_____

_____

Outside the Home 5

Fill in the blank.

1. My friends and I go swimming in the _____.

2. The chimney is on the _____ of our house.

3. I see smoke coming from the _____.

4. Pretty flowers grow in our _____.

5. After I ring the _____, my friend opens
    the door.

6. We have five lawn chairs and a picnic table on our _____.

7. There are two cars parked on our _____.

8. After we park the car in the _____, we close the door.

chimney	roof	patio
garage	driveway	garden
carport	doorbell	swimming pool

Appliances 1

Here are some words for you to use.

freezer	washer	dryer
blender	toaster	radio
oven	vacuum	appliances

Appliances 2

Follow these directions.

underline: freezer   washer

cross out: blender   vacuum

circle: toaster   radio

freezer	washer	dryer	blender	toaster	radio
oven	vacuum	appliances		washer	blender
radio	vacuum	freezer	dryer	blender	radio
oven	appliances	freezer	washer	dryer	blender
appliance	vacuum	oven	radio	toaster	blender
dryer	washer	freezer	appliances	oven	toaster
dryer	freezer	washer	blender	toaster	oven
appliances	freezer	washer		dryer	blender
toaster	radio	oven	vacuum		appliances
vacuum	oven	radio	toaster	blender	dryer
washer	freezer	appliances		oven	toaster
dryer	freezer	vacuum	radio	blender	washer

Appliances 3

Circle the correct answer.

1. Which of these might be very cold?

   a. garden
   b. freezer
   c. napkin
   d. spoon
   e. sink

2. What job can you do with a washer?

   a. wash plates
   b. wash the carpet
   c. wash the driveway
   d. wash towels
   e. wash the VCR

3. Which of these could help you make a milkshake?

   a. blender
   b. vacuum
   c. balcony
   d. garage
   e. elevator

4. Which of these is not an appliance?

   a. washer
   b. dryer
   c. vacuum
   d. swimming pool
   e. toaster

5. Which of these do you use to listen to music?

   a. closet
   b. radio
   c. hall
   d. refrigerator
   e. carport

6. Which of these helps keep our carpet clean?

   a. vacuum
   b. knife
   c. mirror
   d. lamp
   e. attic

7. Which of these helps cook our food?

   a. patio
   b. hall
   c. garden
   d. dishwasher
   e. oven

Appliances 4

Some of the words in this story are spelled wrong. Cross out the 8 mistakes. Write the correct spelling above the mistake. The word list will help you.

This morning Mom went to the kitchen and turned on the radoi. She took a loaf of bread from the frezer. She wanted to make some toast in the taoster. Then she plugged in the belnder to make some juice.

Dad was in the laundry room. He took the wet clothes from the washeer. He put the clothes in the drier. He went upstairs and took the vaccuum out of the closet. He smelled something good in the uven.

Mom said, "Breakfast is ready."

washer	dryer	freezer
vacuum	toaster	radio
blender	appliances	oven

Appliances 5

Follow the directions.

draw:	a toaster on the counter
cross out:	the washer and the dryer
draw:	a radio near the toaster
draw:	a stove
label:	the oven on your stove
draw:	a blender on the counter
circle:	the blender
label:	two more things in the picture

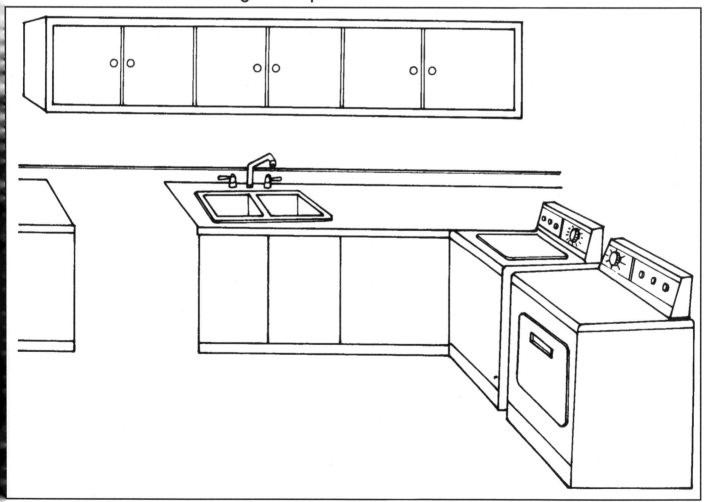

Appliances 6

Fill in the blank.

1. We use the _____ to dry our wet clothes.

2. Keep the frozen food in the _____ .

3. I can hear my favorite song on the _____ .

4. We cooked our turkey in the _____ .

5. We mix things together in the _____ .

6. A blender, toaster, and vacuum are all _____ .

7. Dad washes our dirty clothes in the _____ .

8. It is my job to clean the carpets with the _____ .

radio	appliances	freezer
toaster	oven	vacuum
blender	dryer	washer

Household Items 1

Name:

Here are some words for you to use.

wall unit

china cabinet

coffee table

crib

fireplace

furnace

furniture

toys

end table

Household Items 2

Name:

Underline the correctly spelled words. Then, write the word three times.

Underline		Write
furnase	furnace	_____
furnace	furnice	
furnace	furness	_____
firnace	furnace	_____
fireplace	fireplase	_____
fireplays	fireplace	
fireplace	fireplace	_____
firplace	fireplac	_____
firniture	furniture	_____
furnature	furnitur	
furniture	ferniture	_____
furniture	furniture	_____
cofee table	coffee table	_____
coffe table	coffee tabel	
coffee table	coffee table	_____
coffee table	cofeee table	_____

Household Items 3

Name:

Circle the correct answer.

1. Which of these might be found in a wall unit?
   - a. CD player
   - b. furnace
   - c. shower
   - d. toilet
   - e. couch

2. Which of these might be found in a china cabinet?
   - a. curtains
   - b. toothbrush
   - c. pillow
   - d. plate
   - e. soap

3. Where would you probably find a coffee table?
   - a. bedroom
   - b. living room
   - c. closet
   - d. kitchen
   - e. drawer

4. Which of these might be hot?
   - a. refrigerator
   - b. freezer
   - c. fireplace
   - d. crib
   - e. doorbell

5. Where might a baby sleep?
   - a. alarm clock
   - b. chimney
   - c. crib
   - d. lamp
   - e. mug

6. Which of these is not furniture?
   - a. couch
   - b. armchair
   - c. end table
   - d. bed
   - e. towel

7. On which of these would you put a lamp?
   - a. alarm clock
   - b. glass
   - c. plate
   - d. curtains
   - e. end table

Household Items 4

Name: _____

Complete each sentence.

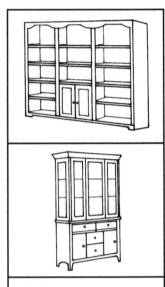

In our home, we sometimes see a _____

_____

In our home, we sometimes see _____

_____

In our home, we sometimes _____

_____

In our home _____

_____

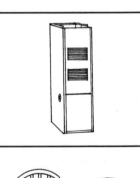

In _____

_____

_____

_____

Household Items 5

Name: _____

Write a sentence using each of these words.

1. end table _____

_____

2. toys _____

_____

3. furniture _____

_____

4. wall unit _____

_____

5. china cabinet _____

_____

6. fireplace _____

_____

7. coffee table _____

_____

8. crib _____

_____

Household Items 6

Name: _____

Fill in the blank.

1. Grandpa tells us to pick up our _____ before we go to bed.

2. There are three logs burning in the _____.

3. The _____ can hold a television and a VCR.

4. Put the lamp on the _____ beside the couch.

5. The baby is sleeping in the _____.

6. We keep our best dishes in the _____ in the dining room.

7. Put your magazines on the _____ in front of the couch.

8. The gas _____ in the basement heats the whole building.

coffee table	furniture	wall unit
furnace	toys	fireplace
end table	china cabinet	crib

Extension Activity 1

Name:

Write each word in the correct box.

fan	piano	bunk bed	ball
coffee maker	doll	toaster	oven
teddy bear	marbles	high chair	can opener
mixer	doll house	dining room table	

Furniture

Appliances

Toys

Extension Activity 2

Make a list for each category.

things kept in a closet

_____   _____

_____   _____

_____   _____

_____   _____

things you write on a calendar

_____   _____

_____   _____

_____   _____

_____   _____

types of rooms in your home

_____   _____

_____   _____

_____   _____

_____   _____

Extension Activity 2

List some people who might visit your home.

Relatives

_____

_____

_____

_____

_____

Friends

_____

_____

_____

_____

_____

Vocabulary Picture Cards

kitchen	refrigerator	stove
microwave	dishwasher	cupboard
sink	drawer	knife
fork	spoon	plate

Vocabulary Picture Cards, cont.

bowl	mug	glass
napkin	living room	couch
armchair	curtains	CD Player
television	lamp	VCR

Vocabulary Picture Cards, cont.

DVD player	bathroom	soap
washcloth	toothbrush	toilet
bedroom	bed	closet
mirror	blanket	dresser

Vocabulary Picture Cards, cont.

pillow

bathtub

shower

towel

alarm clock